Published by The Child's World®
1980 Lookout Drive • Mankato, MN 56003-1705
800-599-READ • www.childsworld.com

Content Consultant: Meri DuRand, CVT, RLATG,
and Veterinary Technician Instructor,
Dakota County Technical College

Photographs ©: iStockphoto, cover, 1, 5, 9, 16, 18, 23, 24, 28; Aspen Rock/Shutterstock Images, 6; Fat Camera/iStockphoto, 10; Jaromir Chalabala/Shutterstock Images, 12; Laura Fay/iStockphoto, 13; Shutterstock Images, 14, 20, 27; Tyler Olson/Shutterstock Images, 15; Dima Sidelnikov/Shutterstock Images, 19

Copyright © 2020 by The Child's World®
All rights reserved. No part of this book may be reproduced or utilized in any form or by any means without written permission from the publisher.

ISBN 9781503835559
LCCN 2019943074

Printed in the United States of America

CONTENTS

FAST FACTS 4

CHAPTER ONE
First Day at the Clinic 7

CHAPTER TWO
Caring for Injured Animals 11

CHAPTER THREE
Calming Scared Pets 17

CHAPTER FOUR
New Client 21

CHAPTER FIVE
Working on a Farm 25

Think About It 29
Glossary 30
To Learn More 31
Selected Bibliography 31
Index 32
About the Author 32

FAST FACTS

What's the Job?
- Veterinary technicians, also known as vet techs or veterinary nurses, assist veterinarians. They help treat animals with injuries or illnesses.
- The minimum education for this job is a two-year associate's degree. After vet techs complete the program, they can take the Veterinary Technician National Exam. Once they pass the exam, they become **credentialed** to work as vet techs.
- Many vet techs work evenings, weekends, or holidays.

Important Stats
- In 2018, there were around 106,680 veterinary technicians and technologists in the United States. Veterinary technologists often do research in a lab.
- In 2018, veterinary technicians and technologists made around $34,420 a year.
- By 2026, this job field is expected to grow by 20 percent. This is faster than most other jobs.

Vet techs often work in animal hospitals or clinics. ▶

CHAPTER ONE

FIRST DAY AT THE CLINIC

A loud beeping woke Amy up before the sun had fully risen. She hit the button on her alarm clock to stop the noise and got out of bed. Today was her first day at an animal clinic. She was a vet tech. Amy knew her education prepared her for this job, but she still felt nervous.

She put on her teal scrubs and tennis shoes. Scrubs are loose-fitting cotton clothes worn by all kinds of doctors and nurses. Tennis shoes were important because Amy knew she would spend lots of time on her feet that day.

Amy's scrubs were not new. She had worn them for many hours while studying to become a vet tech. Remembering the hands-on experience she did at a clinic during school made her feel confident. Vet techs have to complete a two-year program **accredited** by the American Veterinary Medical Association.

◀ **Vet techs treat animals of all ages.**

During the program, they learn about animal medicine, behavior, surgery, and nursing. Then, they take a test to get credentialed. The test had 200 multiple-choice questions, and it took Amy four hours to complete.

Amy left her house. She rode a city bus to the animal clinic. The sunrise turned the sky pink and orange. The bus rolled to a stop. Amy got off and walked to the clinic. The waiting room had a few animals with their owners in it. She heard a quiet meow.

Dr. Jones was one of the veterinarians at the clinic. She wore a white lab coat. Amy's job as a vet tech was to assist Dr. Jones. Together, they would help animals who were sick or injured. While Dr. Jones was busy with surgery or other tasks, Amy helped with ordinary checkups. Her first patient was the cat from the waiting room. She asked the owner about the cat's **feces** to see if it was eating and digesting properly.

Amy had multiple appointments throughout the day. Dr. Jones watched Amy work and answered any questions Amy had. Several patients were cats and dogs. A few were small animals such as hamsters and rabbits. After work, Amy got on the bus to go home. She sat down. The plastic seat was warm from the sun. She thought about her first day. Being a vet tech involved social activity, such as greeting patients and talking to their owners. It also involved lab work, such as handling blood or fecal samples.

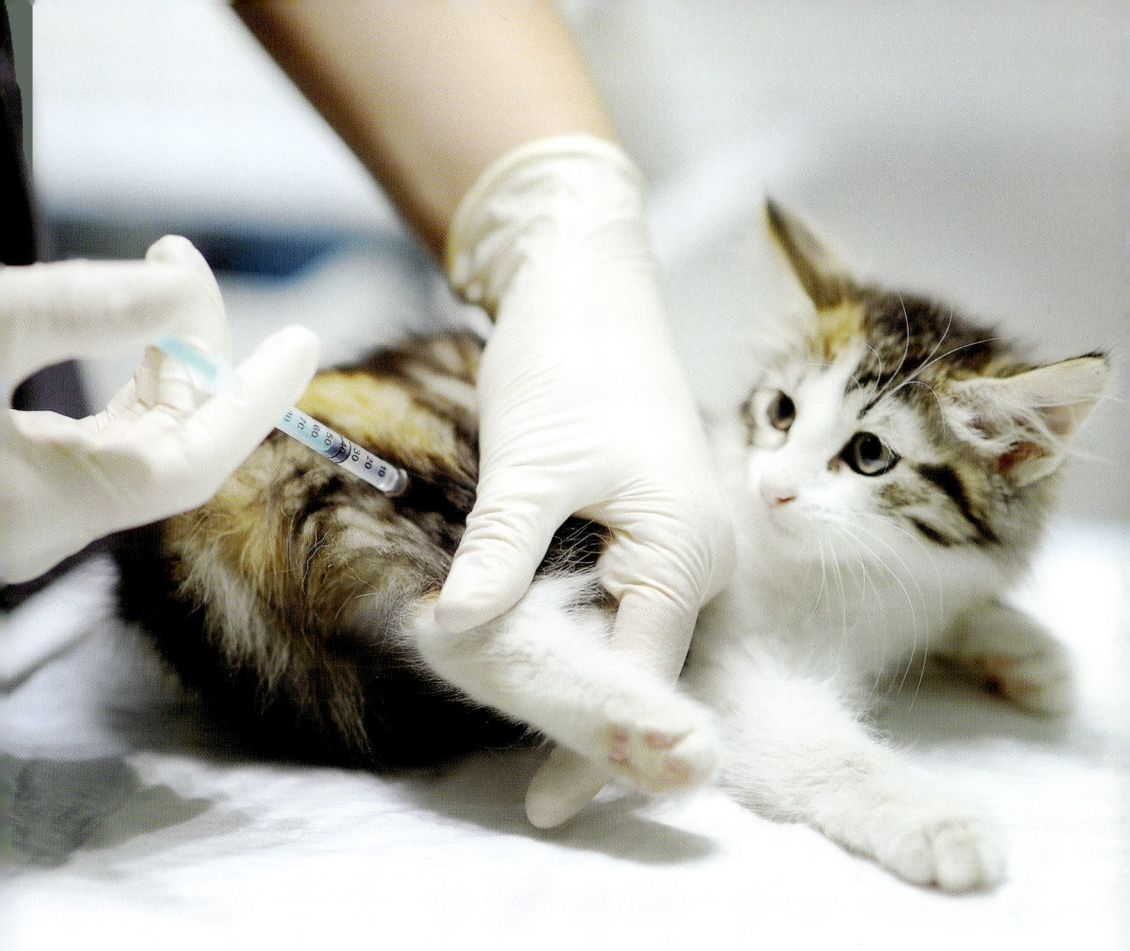

▲ **Vet techs can give animals vaccines and medications.**

Amy couldn't believe how fast the day went. She barely had time to sit down, but this is common for a vet tech. Her first day was tiring, but it was also fun. Amy was excited for work tomorrow.

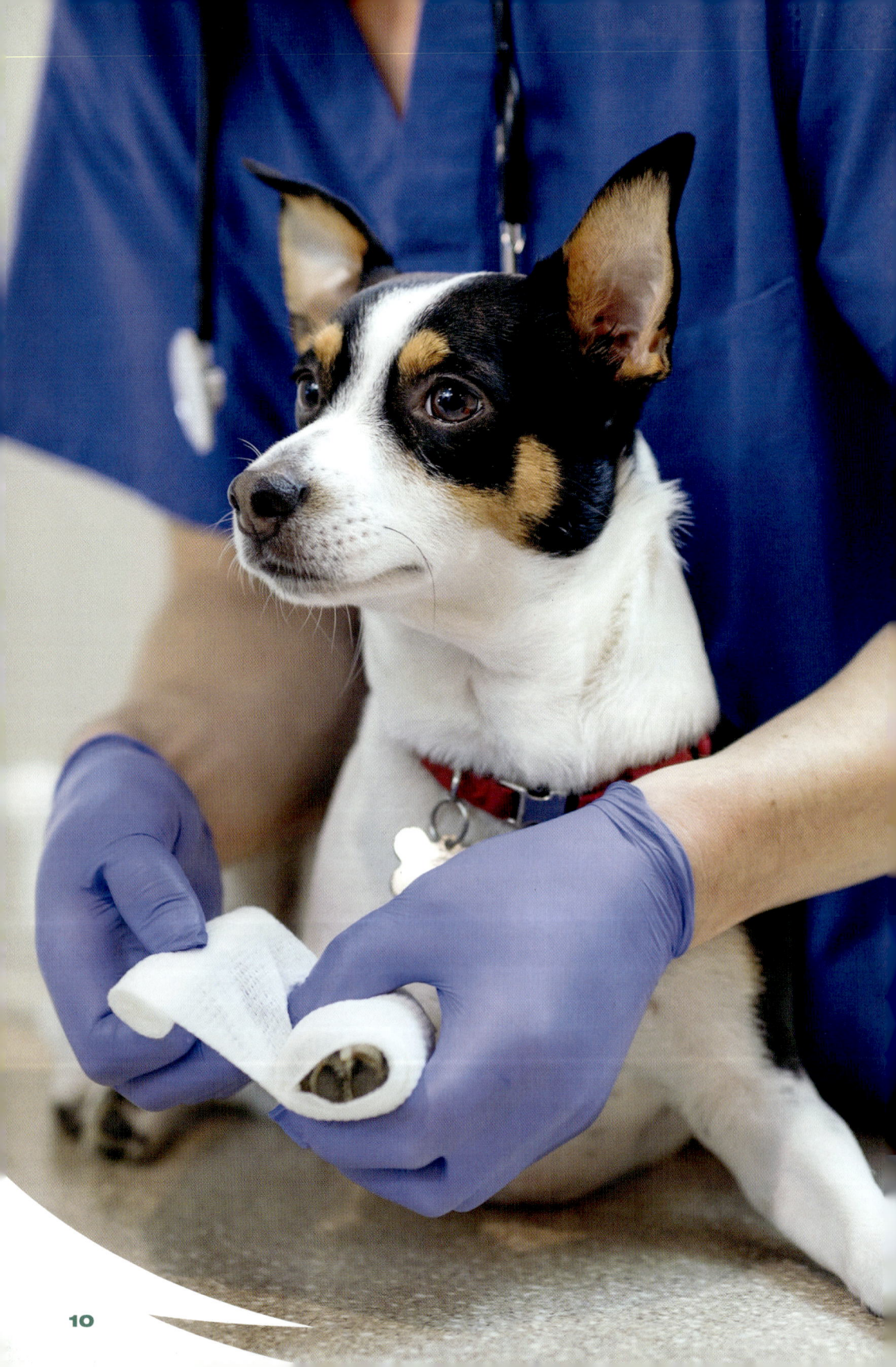

CHAPTER TWO

CARING FOR INJURED ANIMALS

Dave was near the front desk when Liam walked into the vet clinic and closed his umbrella. It was raining hard outside. Next to Liam, his Rottweiler named Juno dripped with water. Juno shook his large body, and water droplets flew on the floor and wall. Dave was a vet tech at the clinic. He led Liam and Juno into an exam room. Liam walked slowly and watched Juno limp beside him on a leg that was bandaged.

Once they were inside the room, Dave closed the door and asked Liam how Juno was doing. Juno had gotten injured while playing on slippery rocks in a river. He had been jumping and running around. At one point, he slipped. A branch cut his skin and went partly into his leg. This was Juno's second appointment after the accident.

◄ **Veterinary professionals need to know how to treat different injuries.**

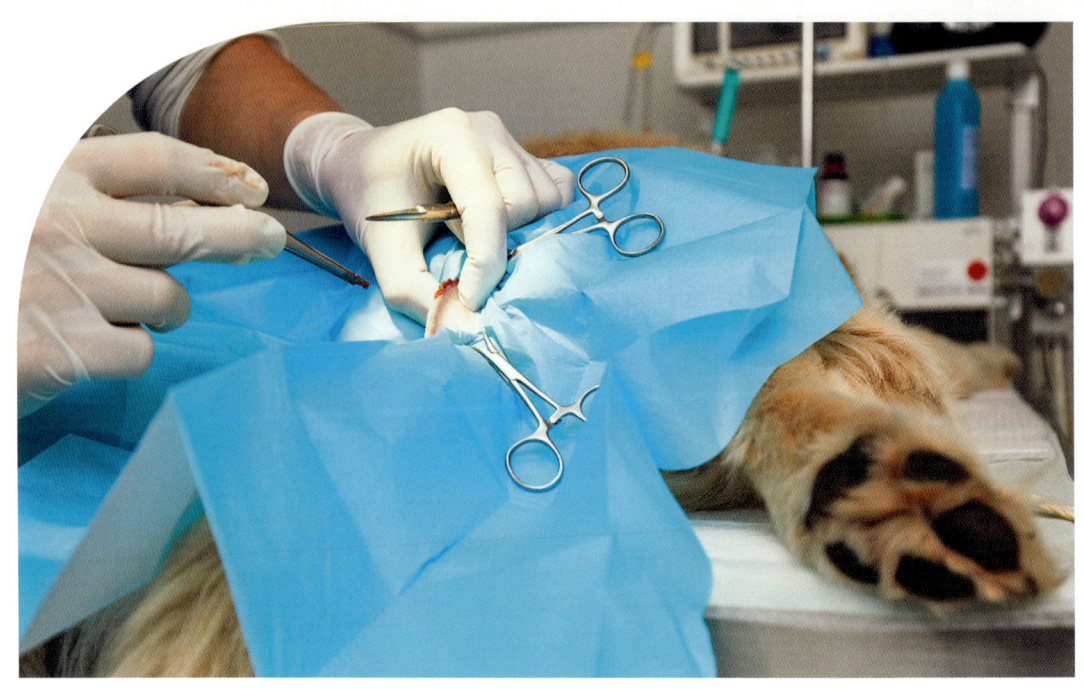

▲ **If injuries are bad, some animals might need surgery.**

Dave went and got fresh bandage supplies. Together, he and the veterinarian would put a new bandage on Juno's leg. The wound needed to be covered with multiple layers of bandaging materials. Otherwise, Juno could lick or pull the bandage off. That would slow the healing process and could lead to an **infection**.

Dave and the veterinarian started putting on the bandaging materials. Having multiple layers added cushion to Juno's injured leg. The final layer of material was stretchy. They wrapped it around Juno's leg to help keep the bandaging in place.

If an animal has an injury that needs to heal, ▶ it might have to wear a cone around its head. This will stop the animal from licking the injury.

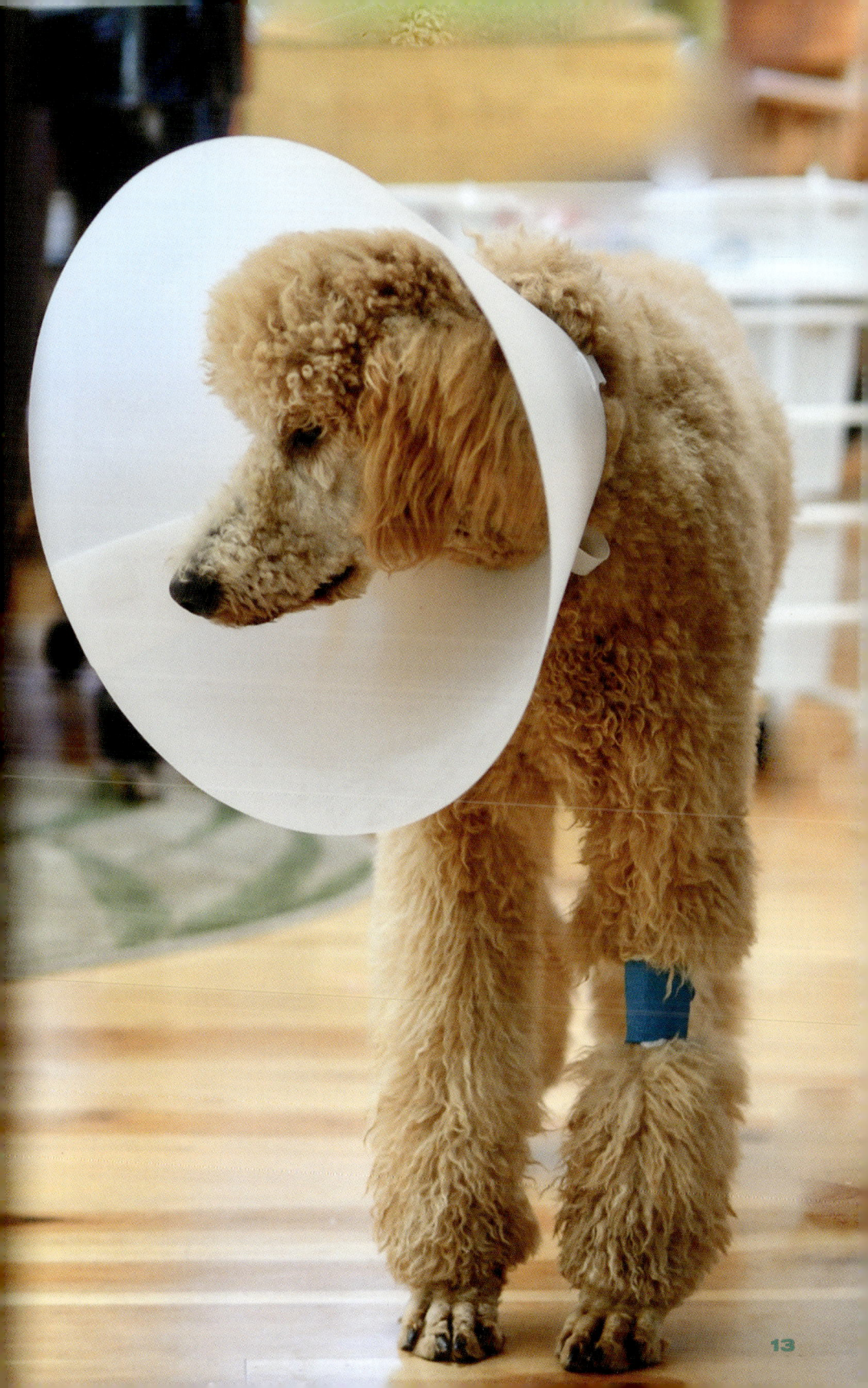

▲ **Sometimes, people mix pills in with an animal's food so the animal eats its medicine at mealtime.**

Juno wiggled during the wrapping process. Both Dave and the veterinarian stayed patient while applying the bandage. If the wound had been swollen, infected, or not scabbing properly, the veterinarian would have told Dave to run tests to make sure everything was okay. But in Juno's case, no additional tests were needed.

▲ **Animal clinic waiting rooms can be filled with pets.**

Juno had been **prescribed** pain medications after the accident. At the end of the appointment, Liam told Dave that his dog didn't want to take the pain medication. Dave suggested coating the pills in food, such as peanut butter. That might make Juno more interested in eating the pills. Dave led Liam and Juno out of the room. They walked down the hall and went to the front desk where the receptionist would check them out. Dave waved goodbye.

CHAPTER THREE

CALMING SCARED PETS

Erin knelt before an orange cat in an exam room. It was in its carrier. Erin was trying to coax it out. The cat raised its paw and lashed out. Its claws scratched Erin's skin, leaving behind long red marks. The cat's owner started to apologize, but Erin shrugged. Minor injuries like that happen as a vet tech. The cat was scared of being in a new place, so it was acting out. Many animals get nervous or **aggressive** while at the vet. Part of being a vet tech is looking for ways to calm the animal.

Instead of trying to take the cat out of its carrier, Erin decided to leave it in. That allowed the cat to stay in a familiar place. It was one way to keep the cat comfortable. Stressed animals can be difficult to deal with. But no matter how many scratches Erin got, she always stayed calm. This helped the animal and owner relax.

◀ **Some animals are curious about new surroundings, and others are cautious.**

▲ **Owners can help calm their pets during visits to the clinic.**

Later, Erin got ready for another appointment. She was organizing files when she heard a bark in the lobby. Erin wondered if it was the dog for her next appointment. She was expecting a Great Dane. Erin saw that it was her next patient and approached the dog slowly. She let it sniff her hand and get used to her smell. She squatted down to be on the same level as the dog. This helped the dog feel less threatened. When animals feel threatened, they may respond by trying to run away or to fight. Erin noticed the faded fur around the dog's eyes. It was a sign of old age.

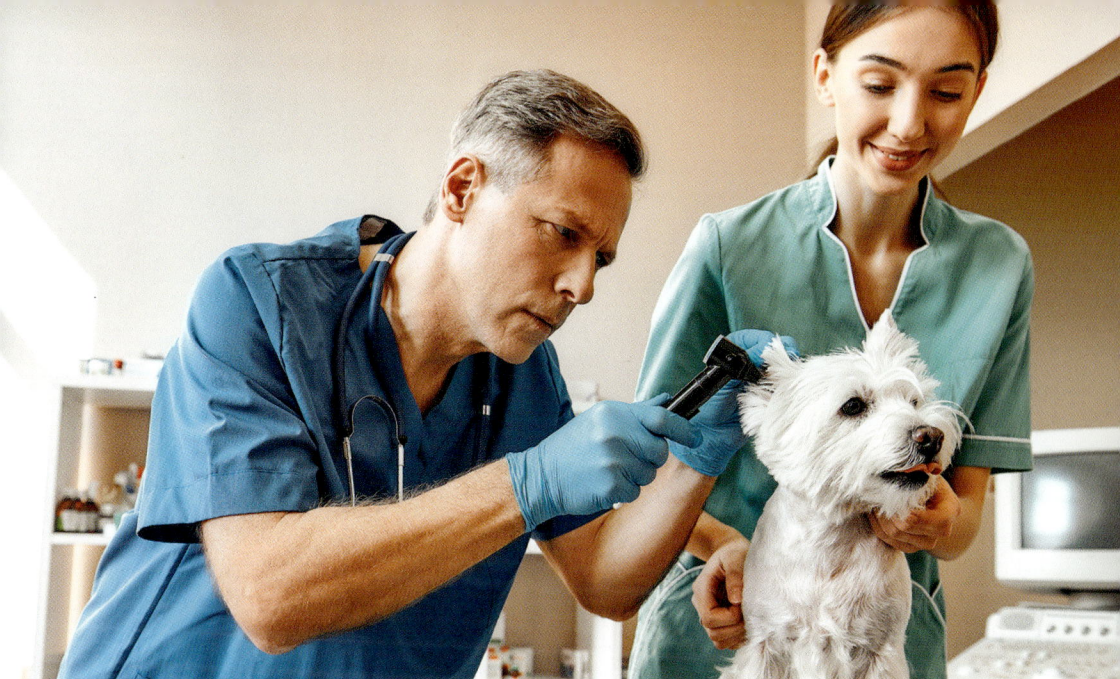

▲ **Vet techs will sometimes hold animals when veterinarians do their exams.**

Erin showed the owner and Great Dane to a room. The owner started to cry as the door closed. It was her last day with her dog. At this appointment, the dog would be **euthanized**. It was old and sick with cancer. Erin was with the owner during the procedure. After, Erin let the owner stay with her dog for as long as she needed. Erin felt bad when owners had to make difficult decisions. For Erin, the physical demands of the job were not as difficult as the emotional ones. Erin took a deep breath. It was sometimes hard being a vet tech, but she couldn't imagine doing anything else.

CHAPTER FOUR

NEW CLIENT

Greg entered the exam room. He washed his hands in the sink and dried them with some paper towels. At the clinic Greg worked at, they sometimes saw **exotic** pets. For Greg's next appointment, he would see a canary. These birds come from tropical islands near the coast of northwest Africa.

The canary had bright yellow feathers. When the owner set the bird's travel cage down, the canary chirped. Greg began asking the owner questions. He needed to record the bird's medical history. That included information such as where the bird came from, its age, and any past illnesses or injuries.

Greg listened to the owner. At the same time, he watched the canary. He observed its behavior and noticed that it was curious. Its head moved quickly from side to side. It looked all around the room. It flew to a new perch.

◀ **Canaries can live for ten or more years if they are healthy.**

Greg asked if the canary had a healthy diet and lots of water. He also asked if the owner had any concerns. The owner didn't. Greg shook hands with the owner and left the room. Next, the veterinarian would do an exam on the bird. The veterinarian might even recommend a more balanced diet for the bird to eat.

Between appointments, Greg helped file records. Medical records keep track of appointment details. A vet needs to consider all parts of an animal's history when making decisions.

During the next appointment, Greg and the vet, Dr. Mill, walked into an exam room. Greg saw a golden lab named Molly resting on the floor by her owner. Molly wagged her tail.

Greg was surprised. Many golden labs have lots of energy. They usually bark or try to jump on him, but Molly was quiet. She was acting different because she had swallowed something she wasn't supposed to. The owner said Molly vomited every time she drank water. Greg talked with Dr. Mill and they came up with a plan. Since Molly couldn't vomit the object out, Dr. Mill ordered an X-ray. An X-ray is a scan of bones and organs. It would help show what was inside Molly's body.

Greg laid Molly on her side and held her still. The X-ray showed that Molly had eaten something large. She wouldn't be able to get rid of it in her feces or vomit it up.

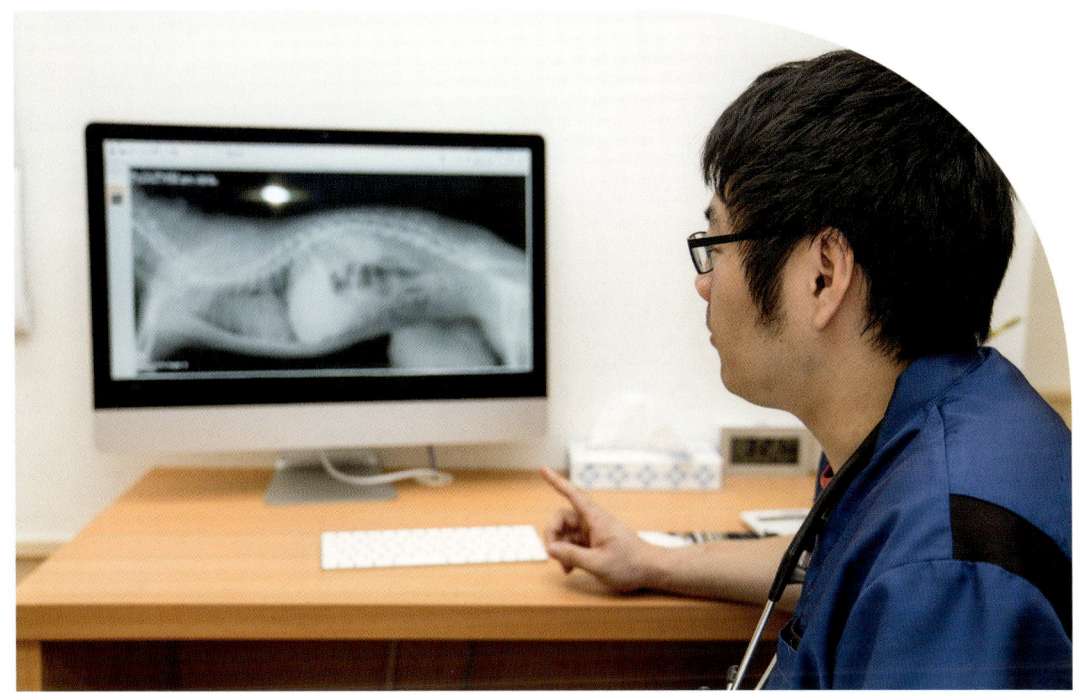

▲ **X-rays can help veterinary professionals figure out if something is wrong inside an animal.**

Dr. Mill decided that Molly needed surgery immediately. She explained the situation to the owner. Before the surgery, Greg got the supplies needed to help Dr. Mill. Greg also gave Molly anesthesia. That medicine made her fall sleep. Molly didn't feel any pain during surgery, and Greg monitored her breathing. Dr. Mill did the surgery. They found that Molly had socks in her stomach. Dr. Mill took them out. Soon, Molly would be eating normally and be full of energy again.

CHAPTER FIVE

WORKING ON A FARM

On Saturday afternoon, Leah arrived at a farm after a drive down a long, winding road. Mud covered the ground, and she felt her rubber boots stick with each step. Leah worked with animals on farms all the time. Many vet techs work odd hours, including nights, weekends, and holidays. Leah was an equine vet tech. That means she specialized in helping horses. Vet techs can choose from many different specialties, such as dentistry, emergency care, or working at a zoo.

Leah saw the horse standing near the barn. Its brown coat shone in the sun. She was at the farm to give it medicine. The owner tried mixing the medicine into the horse's food, but the horse wouldn't eat it. Horses have a good sense of smell and taste. The horse knew the medicine was there.

◀ **Large animal veterinary professionals take care of animals such as cows, horses, goats, sheep, and pigs.**

First, Leah crushed the pills into powder. Then, she mixed the powder with molasses. Molasses is a sweet substance. It is good for hiding the smell and taste of medicine. Also, it is thick, so it wouldn't accidently drip out of the horse's mouth. Leah put the mix into a **syringe** with a large opening. She was ready to give it to the horse. She waved at the owner. Leah wanted him to watch what she did.

Leah walked over and put her hand on the horse's face to say hello. Then, she showed it the syringe. She moved it along its face. Next, she put her thumb under the horse's lip for safety. This let her know where the horse's teeth were. It also helped her get the horse's attention. The horse turned its head to the side. Leah kept her hand on its face. She followed the horse's movements until it was still.

Eventually, the horse opened its mouth. Leah put the syringe as far back as possible. It went over the horse's tongue. She was careful not to poke the horse with the syringe. A quick squeeze shot the medicine mix into the horse's mouth. The horse moved its head up. Leah took her hand away. The horse licked the inside of its mouth clean. The process was a success.

Vet techs can travel to farms to visit animals. ▶

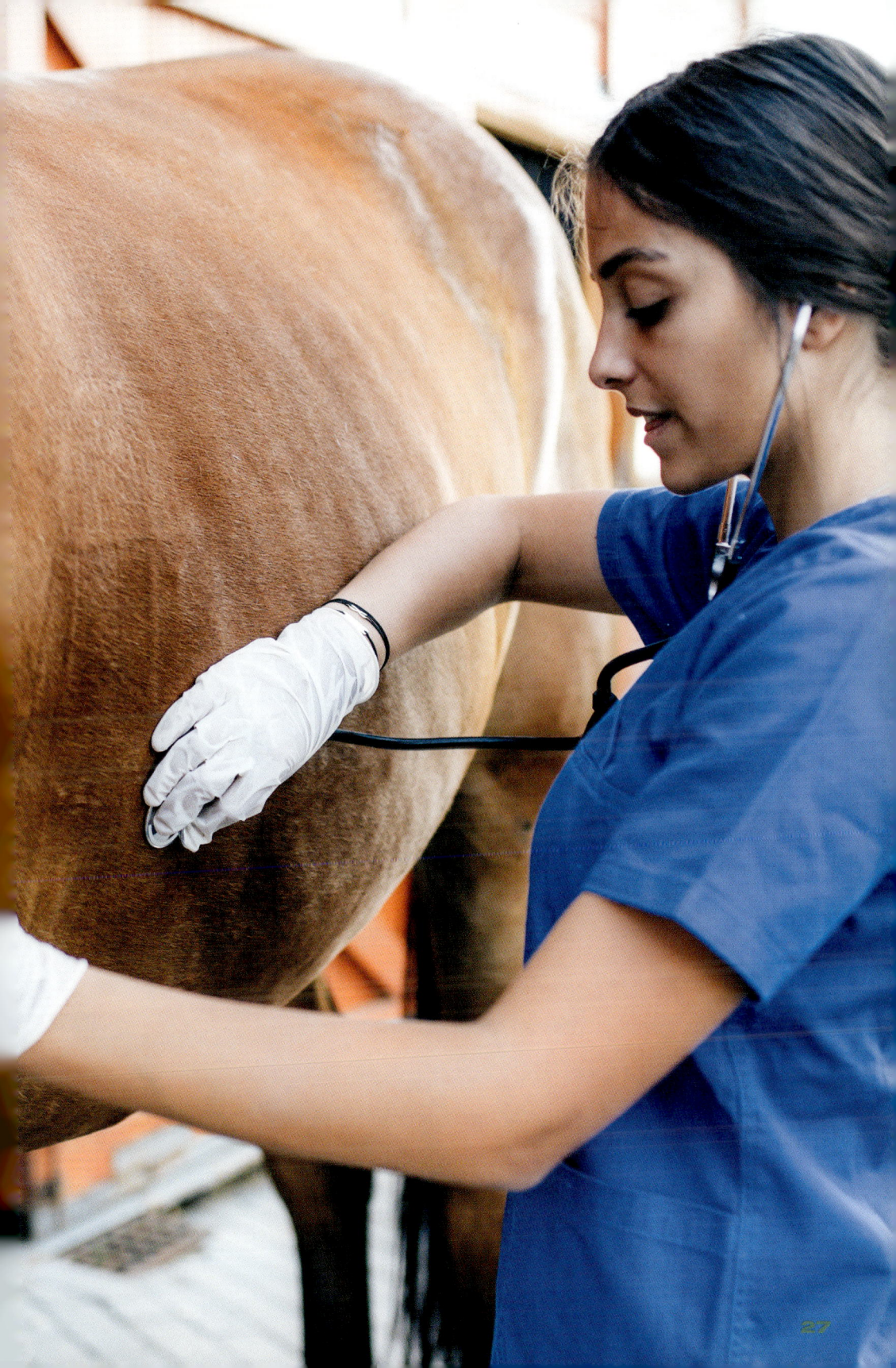

▲ Vet techs can teach owners how to give medicine to their horses.

On her drive home, Leah thought about all the animals she got to help as a vet tech. Sometimes, people asked Leah if she ever wanted to go back to school to become a veterinarian. Leah always shook her head. Vet techs are important members of places such as vet hospitals and clinics, and Leah knew she had chosen the right job for herself.

THINK ABOUT IT

- If you were a vet tech, what types of animals would you want to help? Would you want to specialize in helping certain animals such as horses, birds, or zoo animals? Why or why not?
- Why is it important for vet techs to know how to handle different animals?
- Do you think it's hard for vet techs to deal with sick or injured animals? Explain your answer.

GLOSSARY

accredited (uh-KRED-i-tid): An accredited program has been approved to prepare students for a certain career. Vet techs complete a two-year degree from an accredited school.

aggressive (UH-gress-ive): To be aggressive means to be threatening or violent. The dog was aggressive toward other animals.

credentialed (kri-DEN-shuhld): Credentialed means to have documentation showing experience and qualification. Vet techs need to be credentialed.

euthanized (YOO-thuh-nyzd): When an animal is euthanized, it is killed in a painless way, usually as a last resort. Sometimes old or sick animals are euthanized.

exotic (ig-ZAH-tik): Exotic animals are from another country. Canaries are exotic in the United States.

feces (FEE-seez): Feces is another term for poop. The vet tech looked at the dog's feces to make sure the animal was healthy.

infection (in-FEK-shun): An infection is a situation where bacteria gets inside a wound. Red or puffy wounds are a sign of an infection.

prescribed (pri-SKRIBED): When medical professionals write an order for medicine, that means they have prescribed it for the patient. The veterinarian prescribed pain medication to the injured animal.

syringe (suh-RINJ): A syringe is a handheld device used to administer fluids. Vet techs can use a syringe to give animals medicine.

TO LEARN MORE

BOOKS

Allman, Toney. *Careers If You Like Animals.* San Diego, CA: ReferencePoint Press, 2018.

Bedell, J. M. *So, You Want to Work with Animals?* New York, NY: Aladdin, 2017.

Trueit, Trudi Strain. *Wildlife Conservationist.* New York, NY: Cavendish Square, 2014.

WEBSITES

Visit our website for links about veterinary care: **childsworld.com/links**

Note to Parents, Teachers, and Librarians: We routinely verify our Web links to make sure they are safe and active sites. So encourage your readers to check them out!

SELECTED BIBLIOGRAPHY

"A Day in the Life of a Veterinary Technician." *AAHA*, n.d., aaha.org. Accessed 30 Apr. 2019.

"How to Become a Veterinary Technician: Education & Certification." *All Allied Health Schools*, n.d., allalliedhealthschools.com. Accessed 30 Apr. 2019.

"Veterinary Technologists and Technicians." *Bureau of Labor Statistics*, 29 Mar. 2019, bls.gov. Accessed 30 Apr. 2019.

INDEX

accredited, 7
aggressive, 17
American Veterinary Medical Association, 7
associate's degree, 4

bandage, 11–12, 14

canary, 21–22
cancer, 19
carrier, 17
checkups, 8
clinic, 7–8, 11, 21, 29
credentialed, 4, 8

euthanized, 19
exam room, 11, 17, 21–22
exotic, 21

farm, 25

hamsters, 8

illness, 4, 21
infection, 12, 14
injury, 4, 8, 11–12, 17, 21

medicine, 8, 15, 23, 25–26

rabbits, 8

scabbing, 14
scrubs, 7
surgery, 8, 23
swollen, 14

tennis shoes, 7

Veterinary Technician National Exam, 4

X-ray, 22

ABOUT THE AUTHOR

Emma Huddleston lives in Minnesota with her husband. She enjoys writing children's books, but she likes reading novels even more. When she is not writing or reading, she likes to stay active by running, hiking, and swing dancing.